KS2
9–10
Years

Master Maths at Home

Multiplication and Division

Scan the QR code to help your child's learning at home.

 |

mastermathsathome.com

How to use this book

Maths — No Problem! created **Master Maths at Home** to help children develop fluency in the subject and a rich understanding of core concepts.

Key features of the Master Maths at Home books include:

- Carefully designed lessons that provide structure, but also allow flexibility in how they're used.

- Speech bubbles containing content designed to spark diverse conversations, with many discussion points that don't have obvious 'right' or 'wrong' answers.

- Rich illustrations that will guide children to a discussion of shapes and units of measurement, allowing them to make connections to the wider world around them.

- Exercises that allow a flexible approach and can be adapted to suit any child's cognitive or functional ability.

- Clearly laid-out pages that encourage children to practise a range of higher-order skills.

- A community of friendly and relatable characters who introduce each lesson and come along as your child progresses through the series.

You can see more guidance on how to use these books at **mastermathsathome.com**.

We're excited to share all the ways you can learn maths!

Copyright © 2022 Maths — No Problem!
Maths — No Problem!
mastermathsathome.com
www.mathsnoproblem.com
hello@mathsnoproblem.com

First published in Great Britain in 2022 by
Dorling Kindersley Limited
One Embassy Gardens, 8 Viaduct Gardens, London SW11 7BW
A Penguin Random House Company

The authorised representative in the EEA is Dorling Kindersley
Verlag GmbH. Arnulfstr. 124, 80636 Munich, Germany

10 9 8 7 6 5 4 3 2 1
001–327097–May/22

This book was made with Forest Stewardship Council™ certified paper – one small step in DK's commitment to a sustainable future. For more information go to www.dk.com/our-green-pledge

All rights reserved. Without limiting the rights under the copyright reserved above, no part of this publication may be reproduced, stored in, or introduced into a retrieval system, or transmitted, in any form, or by any means (electronic, mechanical, photocopying, recording, or otherwise), without the prior written permission of the copyright owner.

A CIP catalogue record for this book is available from the British Library.

ISBN: 978-0-24153-942-2
Printed and bound in the UK

For the curious
www.dk.com

Acknowledgements

The publisher would like to thank the authors and consultants Andy Psarianos, Judy Hornigold, Adam Gifford and Dr Anne Hermanson.

The Castledown typeface has been used with permission from the Colophon Foundry.

Contents

	Page
Multiples	4
Factors	6
Common factors	8
Composite, square and prime numbers	10
Square numbers	12
Cube numbers	14
Multiplying by 10, 100 and 1000	16
Multiplying 2- and 3-digit numbers	18
Multiplying 4-digit numbers (part 1)	22
Multiplying 4-digit numbers (part 2)	26
Multiplying 2-digit by 2-digit numbers (part 1)	30
Multiplying 2-digit by 2-digit numbers (part 2)	32
Dividing by 10, 100 and 1000	34
Dividing 3-digit numbers	36
Dividing 4-digit numbers	38
Dividing with remainder	42
Review and challenge	44
Answers	46

Ruby   Elliott   Amira   Charles   Lulu   Sam   Oak   Holly   Ravi   Emma   Jacob   Hannah

Multiples

Lesson 1

Starter

Ravi can count in eights.

8, 16, 24, 32, 40, 48, 56, 64, 72, 80

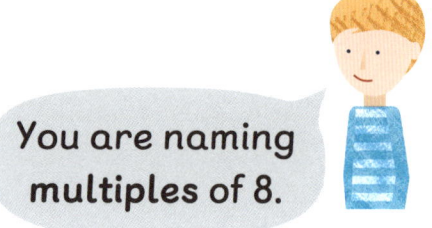

You are naming multiples of 8.

What does Sam mean?

Example

We can describe multiples of 8 as numbers that divide exactly by 8.
When we multiply a whole number by 8, the product is also a multiple of 8.

1 × 8 = 8
2 × 8 = 16
3 × 8 = 24
4 × 8 = 32
5 × 8 = 40
6 × 8 = 48
7 × 8 = 56
8 × 8 = 64
9 × 8 = 72
10 × 8 = 80
11 × 8 = 88
12 × 8 = 96

1	2	3	4	5	6	7	8	9	10
11	12	13	14	15	16	17	18	19	20
21	22	23	24	25	26	27	28	29	30
31	32	33	34	35	36	37	38	39	40
41	42	43	44	45	46	47	48	49	50
51	52	53	54	55	56	57	58	59	60
61	62	63	64	65	66	67	68	69	70
71	72	73	74	75	76	77	78	79	80
81	82	83	84	85	86	87	88	89	90
91	92	93	94	95	96	97	98	99	100

The orange numbers on the 100-square are all multiples of 8.

Practice

1 (a) Draw a circle around each multiple of 3.

(b) Draw a square around each multiple of 7.

1	2	3	4	5	6	7	8	9	10
11	12	13	14	15	16	17	18	19	20
21	22	23	24	25	26	27	28	29	30
31	32	33	34	35	36	37	38	39	40
41	42	43	44	45	46	47	48	49	50
51	52	53	54	55	56	57	58	59	60
61	62	63	64	65	66	67	68	69	70
71	72	73	74	75	76	77	78	79	80
81	82	83	84	85	86	87	88	89	90
91	92	93	94	95	96	97	98	99	100

2 Fill in the blanks with the missing multiples.

(a) Multiples of 4:

4, 8, ____, 16, ____, ____, ____, 32, 36, ____, ____, ____, ...

(b) Multiples of 6:

6, ____, ____, 24, ____, ____, ____, ____, 54, 60, ____, ____, ...

3 Fill in the blanks. The first one has been done for you.

(a) 8 is a multiple of 1, 2, 4 and 8.

(b) 6 is a multiple of 1, ____, ____ and ____.

(c) 10 is a multiple of ____, ____, ____ and ____.

5

Factors

Lesson 2

Starter

Ruby and Charles are playing a card game. Each row must have the same number of cards.
How many ways can Ruby and Charles arrange the cards?

Example

Ruby and Charles can arrange the cards in a single row.

There is 1 row of 12 cards.

1 × 12 = 12

We say that 1 and 12 are factors of 12.

They can arrange the cards into 2 rows of 6.

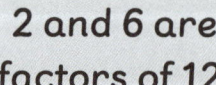

2 × 6 = 12

2 and 6 are factors of 12.

They can leave the cards as 3 rows of 4.

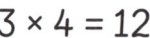

3 × 4 = 12

3 and 4 are factors of 12.

We can say that all the factors of 12 are 1, 2, 3, 4, 6 and 12.

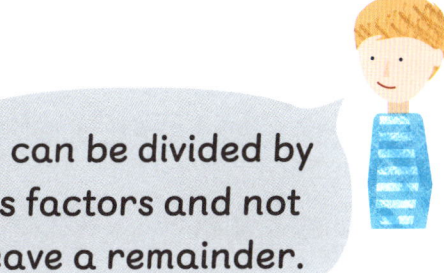

12 can be divided by its factors and not leave a remainder.

Practice

Fill in the blanks.

1 (a) ☐ × 1 = 8   ☐ × 2 = 8

☐ × 4 = 8   ☐ × 8 = 8

The factors of 8 are ☐ , ☐ , ☐ and ☐ .

(b) ☐ × 1 = 14   ☐ × 2 = 14

☐ × 7 = 14   ☐ × 14 = 14

The factors of 14 are ☐ , ☐ , ☐ and ☐ .

(c) ☐ × ☐ = 21   ☐ × ☐ = 21

The factors of 21 are ☐ , ☐ , ☐ and ☐ .

2 (a) The factors of 18 are ☐ , ☐ , ☐ , ☐ , ☐

and ☐ .

(b) The factors of 16 are ☐ , ☐ , ☐ , ☐

and ☐ .

Common factors

Lesson 3

Starter

Which numbers are factors of both 10 and 15?

Example

1 is a factor of all whole numbers.

1 × 10 = 10   2 × 5 = 10

The factors of 10 are 1, 2, 5 and 10.

1 × 15 = 15   3 × 5 = 15

The factors of 15 are 1, 3, 5 and 15.

1 and 5 are common factors of 10 and 15.

This means if we divide 10 or 15 by 1 or 5, we will not be left with a remainder.

Find the common factors of 6 and 18.

1 × 6 = 6   1 × 18 = 18
2 × 3 = 6   2 × 9 = 18
                  3 × 6 = 18

The factors of 6 are 1, 2, 3 and 6.

The factors of 18 are 1, 2, 3, 6, 9 and 18.

The common factors of 6 and 18 are 1, 2, 3 and 6.

Both numbers can be divided by 1, 2, 3 and 6 and not leave a remainder.

Practice

1 Fill in the blanks.

(a) The factors of 24 are ☐ , ☐ , ☐ , ☐ , ☐ , ☐ , ☐ and ☐ .

(b) The factors of 32 are ☐ , ☐ , ☐ , ☐ , ☐ and ☐ .

(c) The common factors of 24 and 32 are ☐ , ☐ , ☐ and ☐ .

2 Find three numbers that have the following common factors.

(a) 2, 4, 8   ☐ , ☐ , ☐

(b) 3, 5, 10   ☐ , ☐ , ☐

Composite, square and prime numbers

Lesson 4

Starter

Lulu found the factors for 6, 4 and 3. What does the number of factors tell us about the number?

The factors of 6 are 1, 2, 3 and 6.
The factors of 4 are 1, 2 and 4.
The factors of 3 are 1 and 3.

Example

The number 6 has 4 factors.
The factors of 6 are 1, 2, 3 and 6.

We can make a rectangle using 1 row of 6.

1 × 6 = 6

We can make a rectangle using 2 rows of 3.

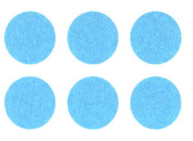

2 × 3 = 6

When a number has more than 2 factors we call it a **composite number**.

The number 4 has 3 factors.
The factors of 4 are 1, 2 and 4.

We can make a rectangle using 1 row of 4.

1 × 4 = 4

We can also make a square using 2 rows of 2.

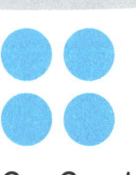

2 × 2 = 4

 We say that 4 is a square number.

  Square numbers have an odd number of factors.

We can write $2 \times 2 = 2^2$.

We read 2^2 as 2 squared.

The number 3 has 2 factors.
The factors of 3 are 1 and 3.

 We can only make a rectangle using a single row.

$1 \times 3 = 3$

 3 is a prime number.

 A prime number has only 2 factors, 1 and itself.

Practice

1 Find the factors of the following numbers.

(a) The factors of 8 are _____.

(b) The factors of 16 are _____.

(c) The factors of 13 are _____.

2 List three numbers that are prime numbers.

☐ , ☐ , ☐

3 List three numbers that have an odd number of factors.

☐ , ☐ , ☐

11

Square numbers

Lesson 5

Starter

Jacob made the following patterns using tiles.

How many tiles does he need to make the next square?

Example

This square is made from 1 row of 1.

$1 \times 1 = 1^2$

We read 1^2 as 1 squared.

1 is a square number.

This square is made from 2 rows of 2.

$2 \times 2 = 4$
$2 \times 2 = 2^2$

4 is a square number.

$3 \times 3 = 9$
$3 \times 3 = 3^2$
9 is a square number.

We can use 4^2 or 4×4 to find the number of tiles Jacob needs to make the next square.

$4^2 = 4 \times 4$
$= 16$

The numbers 1, 4, 9 and 16 are square numbers.

Practice

1 Fill in the blanks to find the square numbers. The first two have been done for you.

(a) $1^2 = 1 \times 1 = 1$

(b) $2^2 = 2 \times 2 = 4$

(c) $3^2 = 3 \times 3 = \boxed{}$

(d) $4^2 = \boxed{} \times \boxed{} = \boxed{}$

(e) $5^2 = \boxed{} \times \boxed{} = \boxed{}$

(f) $8^2 = \boxed{} \times \boxed{} = \boxed{}$

(g) $10^2 = \boxed{} \times \boxed{} = \boxed{}$

Cube numbers

Lesson 6

Starter

How can Emma describe the shape she has made?

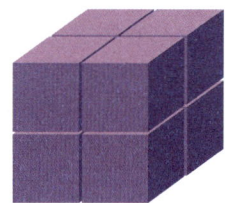

Example

We can describe the length, width and height of this cube as 2 × 2 × 2.

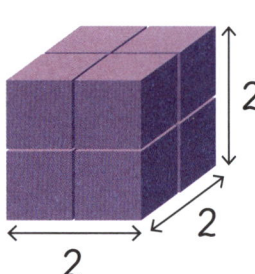

We say that 2^3 is a cube number.

$2 \times 2 \times 2 = 2^3$
$= 8$

We can describe the length, width and height of this cube as 3 × 3 × 3.

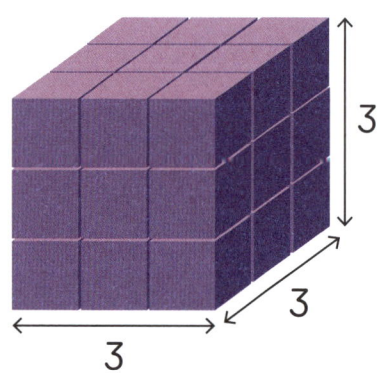

3^3 is a cube number.

$3 \times 3 \times 3 = 3^3$
$= 27$

Practice

1 Find the number of smaller cubes needed to make this large cube.

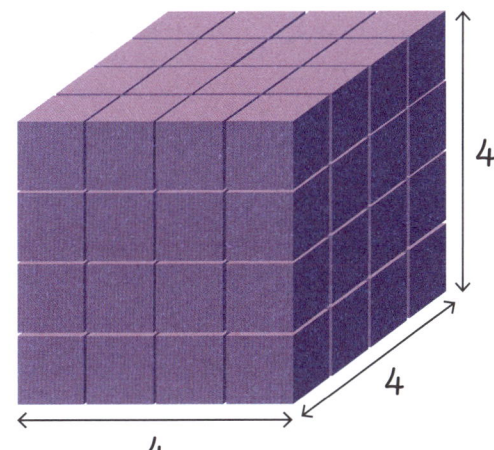

[ ] × [ ] × [ ] = 4^3

= [ ]

There are [ ] smaller cubes in this large cube.

2 Fill in the blanks.

(a) 1^3 = [ ] × [ ] × [ ] = [ ]

(b) 2^3 = [ ] × [ ] × [ ] = [ ]

(c) 3^3 = [ ] × [ ] × [ ] = [ ]

(d) 4^3 = [ ] × [ ] × [ ] = [ ]

(e) 5^3 = [ ] × [ ] × [ ] = [ ]

(f) 6^3 = [ ] × [ ] × [ ] = [ ]

Multiplying by 10, 100 and 1000

Lesson 7

Starter

The depth of a pool is 2 m.
The depth of a river is 10 times greater than the depth of the pool.
The depth of a lake is 100 times greater than the depth of the pool.
The depth of an ocean is 1000 times greater than the depth of the pool.

What is the depth of the river, lake and ocean?

Example

th	h	t	o
			2

× 10 →

th	h	t	o
		2	0

2 × 10 = 20

 20 is 10 times greater than 2.

2 × 1 ten = 2 tens

The depth of the river is 20 m.

th	h	t	o
			2

× 100 →

th	h	t	o
	2	0	0

2 × 100 = 200

16

 20 is 10 times greater than 2.
200 is 100 times greater than 2.

 2 × 1 hundred = 2 hundred

The depth of the lake is 200 m.

th	h	t	o
			2

× 1000 →

th	h	t	o
2	0	0	0

2000 is 1000 times greater than 2.

The depth of the ocean is 2000 m.

Practice

1 Complete the place-value charts and fill in the blanks.

(a) 7 × 100 = ☐

th	h	t	o
			7

× 100 →

th	h	t	o

(b) 9 × 1000 = ☐

th	h	t	o
			9

× 1000 →

th	h	t	o

2 Fill in the blanks.

(a) 13 × 10 = ☐

(b) 27 × ☐ = 2700

(c) 14 × 1000 = ☐

(d) 234 × ☐ = 234 000

17

Multiplying 2- and 3-digit numbers

Lesson 8

Starter

The school buys 8 packets and 6 boxes of paper cups for the school fair. Each packet has 14 cups. Each box has 126 cups.
How many cups are there for the school fair altogether?

Example

Find the number of cups in 8 packets.

```
      1   4
  ×       8
  ─────────
      3   2
```

Start by multiplying the ones.

 4 × 8 = 32

 10 × 8 = 80

```
      1   4
  ×       8
  ─────────
      3   2
  +   8   0
  ─────────
  1   1   2
```

Multiply the tens.

14 × 8 = 112
There are 112 cups in 8 packets.

Find the number of cups in 6 boxes.

```
    1  2  6
 ×        6
 ─────────
       3  6
```

Multiply the ones.

6 × 6 = 36

2 tens × 6 = 12 tens
= 120

20 × 6 = 120

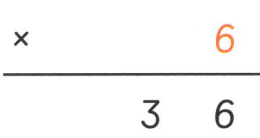

```
    1  2  6
 ×        6
 ─────────
       3  6
    1  2  0
```

Multiply the tens.

100 × 6 = 600

```
    1  2  6
 ×        6
 ─────────
       3  6
    1  2  0
 +  6  0  0
 ─────────
    7  5  6
```

Multiply the hundreds.

126 × 6 = 756

There are 756 cups in 6 boxes.

112 + 756 = 868

There are 868 cups for the school fair altogether.

19

Practice

1 Multiply and fill in the blanks.

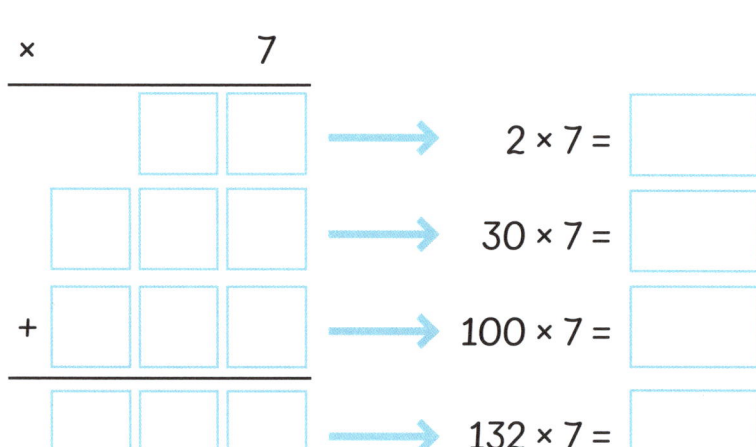

2 Multiply and fill in the blanks.

(a) 147 × 3 = ☐

```
    1  4  7
×         3
―――――――――――
   ☐  ☐
☐  ☐  ☐
+☐ ☐  ☐
―――――――――――
☐  ☐  ☐
```

(b) 216 × 4 = ☐

```
    2  1  6
×         4
―――――――――――
   ☐  ☐
☐  ☐  ☐
+☐ ☐  ☐
―――――――――――
☐  ☐  ☐
```

3 A garden centre uses 165 l of water every day during the summer. What is the total volume of water that the garden centre uses in a week?

The garden centre uses ☐ l of water in a week.

4 A train travelling to Birmingham is full. Each carriage contains 146 passengers. If there are 8 carriages, how many passengers are on the train altogether?

There are ☐ passengers on the train altogether.

Multiplying 4-digit numbers (part 1)

Lesson 9

Starter

Amira's dad's bicycle cost £1232. Amira's mum's bicycle cost twice as much as Amira's dad's bicycle.
What is the total cost of the 2 bicycles?

Example

1 unit is equal to £1232. Find the value of 3 units.

£1232 × 3 = ?

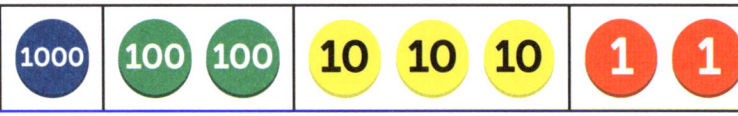

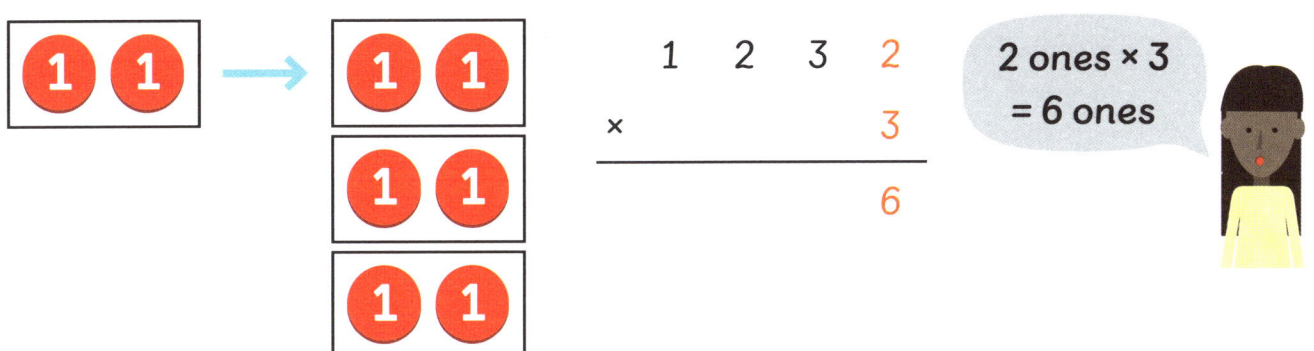
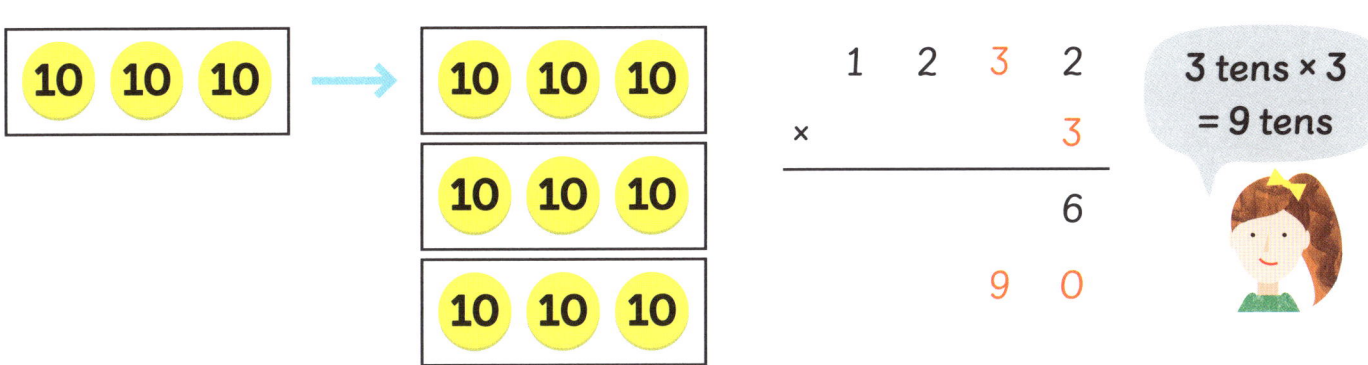
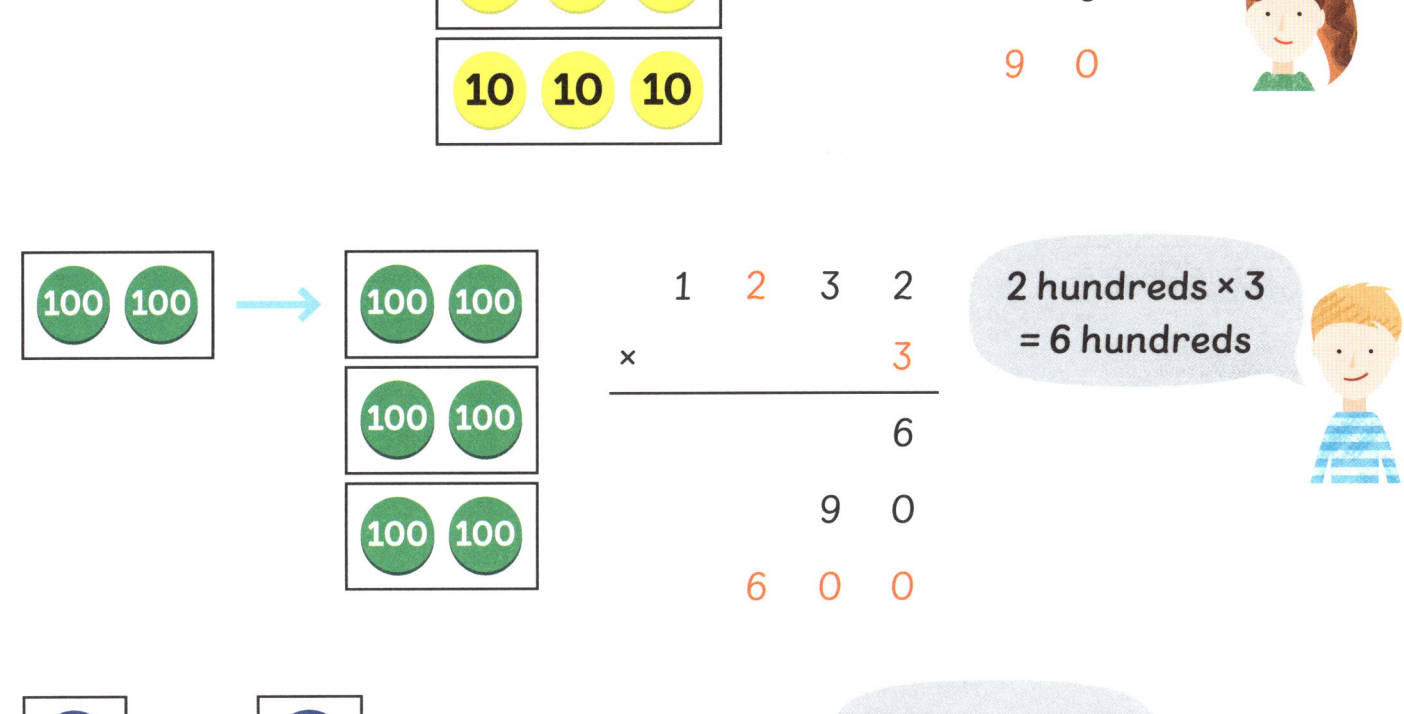
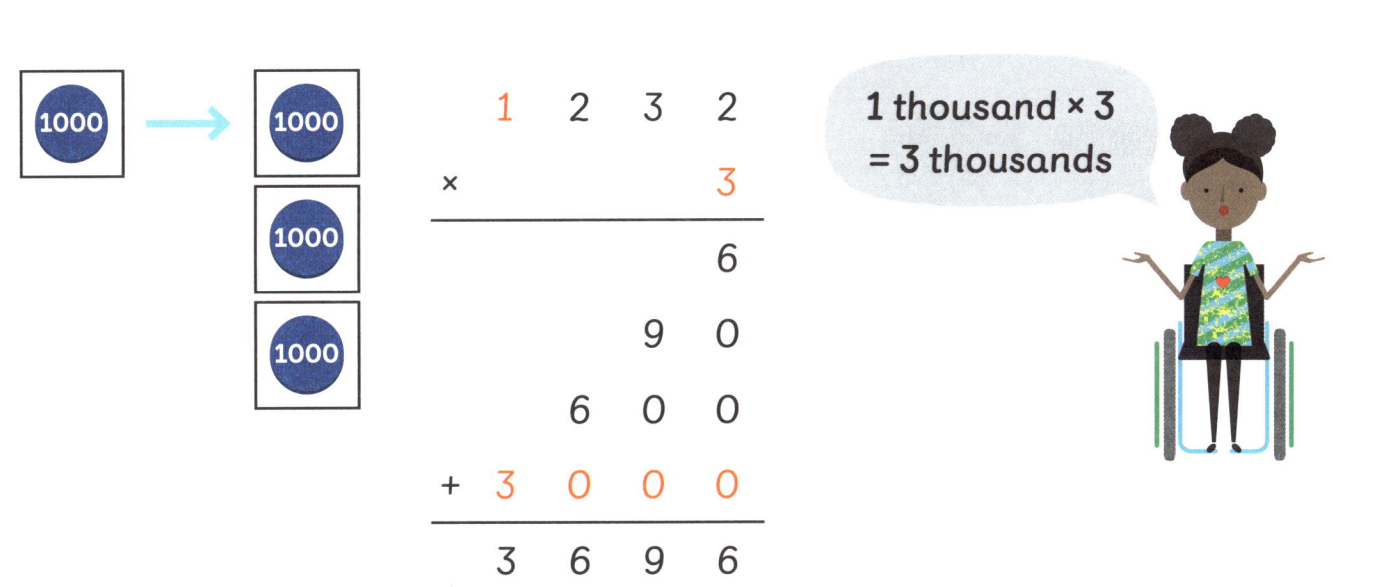

```
    1   2   3   2
×               3
―――――――――――――――――
                6    →    2 × 3 =       6
                9   0    →    30 × 3 =      90
            6   0   0    →    200 × 3 =    600
+   3   0   0   0    →    1000 × 3 =   3000
―――――――――――――――――
    3   6   9   6    →    1232 × 3 =   3696
```

1 unit = £1232
3 units = £1232 × 3
       = £3696

The total cost of the 2 bicycles is £3696.

Practice

1 Multiply.

(a) 2131 × 2 = ☐

1 × 2 = ☐

30 × 2 = ☐

100 × 2 = ☐

2000 × 2 = ☐

(b) 3123 × 3 = ☐

3 × 3 = ☐

20 × 3 = ☐

100 × 3 = ☐

3000 × 3 = ☐

2 Multiply.

(a) 2122 × 4 = ☐

```
      2   1   2   2
  ×               4
  ─────────────────
              ☐
          ☐  ☐
      ☐  ☐  ☐
+ ☐  ☐  ☐  ☐
  ─────────────────
  ☐  ☐  ☐  ☐
```

(b) 3323 × 3 = ☐

```
      3   3   2   3
  ×               3
  ─────────────────
              ☐
          ☐  ☐
      ☐  ☐  ☐
+ ☐  ☐  ☐  ☐
  ─────────────────
  ☐  ☐  ☐  ☐
```

3 Find the product.

(a) 1223 × 3 = ☐

(b) 4233 × 2 = ☐

(c) 3021 × 3 = ☐

(d) 2012 × 4 = ☐

Multiplying 4-digit numbers (part 2)

Lesson 10

Starter

A hotel in Dubai, UAE, had 1348 people staying for 1 week.
Every morning each guest had breakfast.
How many breakfasts were made over the week?

Example

1348 × 7 = ☐

1 week is 7 days.

```
      1  3  4  8
   ×           7
   ─────────────
            5  6   →   8 × 7 =    56
         2  8  0   →   40 × 7 =   280
      2  1  0  0   →   300 × 7 =  2100
   +  7  0  0  0   →   1000 × 7 = 7000
   ─────────────      ─────────────────
      9  4  3  6   →   1348 × 7 = 9436
```

26

$$\begin{array}{r} 1\ \ 3\ \ \overset{5}{4}\ \ 8 \\ \times\ \ \ \ \ \ \ \ \ \ 7 \\ \hline 6 \end{array}$$

8 ones × 7 = 56 ones

Rename 56 ones as 5 tens and 6 ones.

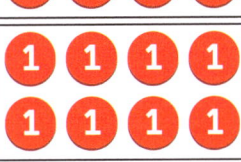

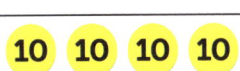 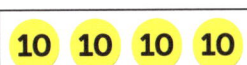

$$\begin{array}{r} 1\ \ \overset{3}{3}\ \ \overset{5}{4}\ \ 8 \\ \times\ \ \ \ \ \ \ \ \ \ 7 \\ \hline 3\ \ 6 \end{array}$$

Rename 33 tens as 3 hundreds and 3 tens.

4 tens × 7 = 28 tens

28 tens + 5 tens = 33 tens

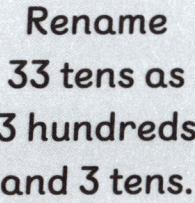

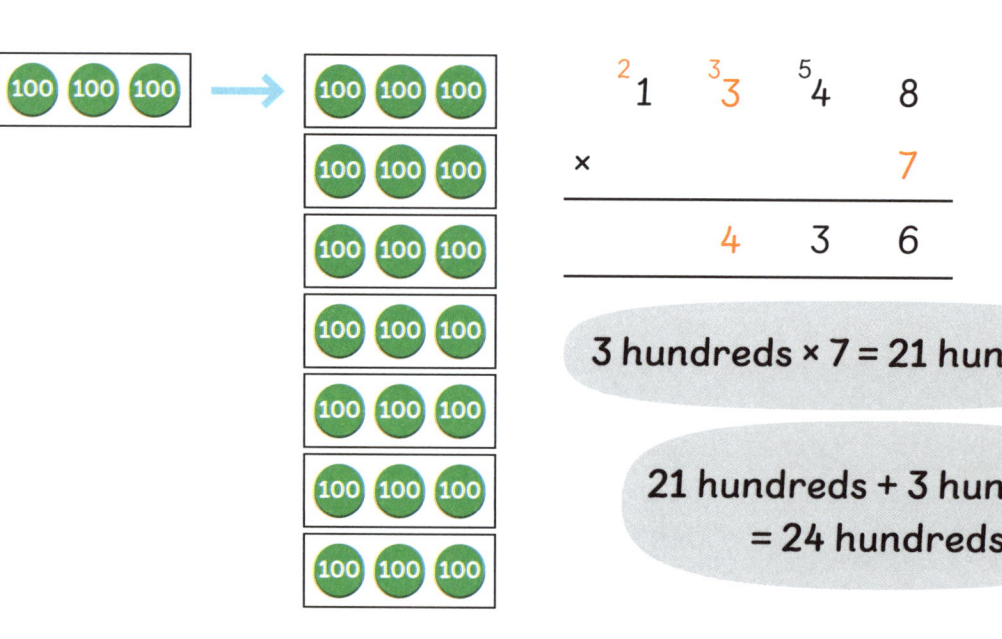

3 hundreds × 7 = 21 hundreds

21 hundreds + 3 hundreds = 24 hundreds

Rename 24 hundreds as 2 thousands and 4 hundreds.

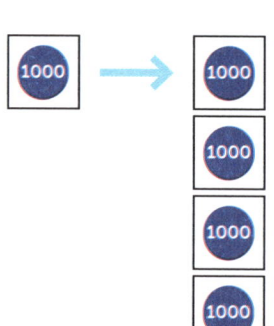

1 thousand × 7 = 7 thousands

7 thousands + 2 thousands = 9 thousands

1348 × 7 = 9436

There were 9436 breakfasts made over the week.

Practice

Multiply.

1 (a) 1426 × 3 = ☐

 1000 × 3 = ☐

 400 × 3 = ☐

 20 × 3 = ☐

 6 × 3 = ☐

(b) 2571 × 4 = ☐

 2000 × 4 = ☐

 500 × 4 = ☐

 70 × 4 = ☐

 1 × 4 = ☐

2 (a) 1 8 3 9
      ×   6
      ─────────

(b) 2 1 7 4
      ×   7
      ─────────

3 There are 6 empty shipping containers loaded onto a ship. If the mass of an empty shipping container is 1987 kg, what is the total mass of the 6 containers being loaded onto the ship?

The total mass of the 6 containers is ☐ kg.

Multiplying 2-digit by 2-digit numbers (part 1)

Lesson 11

Starter

Inside a restaurant there are 11 tables. There are 14 diners at each table. How many diners are there in the restaurant?

Example

4 × 11 = ?

We can break 11 into 1 ten and 1 one.

Multiply 14 by 1 and then by 10.

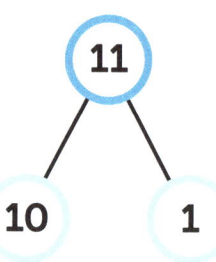

14 × 1 = 14
14 × 10 = 140
14 × 11 = 154

There are 154 diners at the restaurant.

At another restaurant there are 23 tables with 12 diners at each table.

12 = 10 + 2

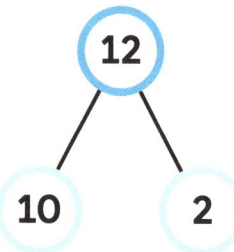

I can start by doubling 23.
23 × 2 = 46

23 × 10 = 230
23 × 2 = 46
23 × 12 = 276

230 + 46 = 276

There are 276 diners at the restaurant.

Practice

Multiply.

1 (a) 31 × 11 = ☐

31 × 1 = ☐

31 × 10 = ☐

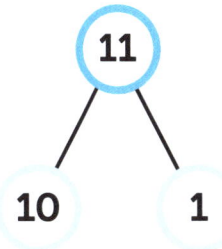

(b) 23 × 13 = ☐

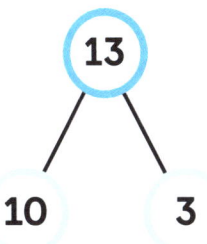

2 (a) 44 × 12 = ☐   (b) 33 × 22 = ☐

Multiplying 2-digit by 2-digit numbers (part 2)

Lesson 12

Starter

A florist makes 37 bouquets of roses to sell in his shop. He uses 24 roses to make each bouquet.
How many roses does he use altogether to make the bouquets?

Example

$37 \times 24 = ?$

Start by multiplying 37 by 4.

3 tens × 4 = 12 tens

```
    ²3   7
 ×   2   4
 ─────────
         8
```

```
    ²3   7
 ×   2   4
 ─────────
     1 4 8
```

12 tens + 2 tens = 14 tens

7 ones × 4 = 28 ones

2 tens × 30 = 60 tens

```
  1
    ²3   7
 ×   2   4
 ─────────
     1 4 8
         4
```

```
  1
    ²3   7
 ×   2   4
 ─────────
     1 4 8
 +   7 4
 ─────────
     8 8 8
```

60 tens = 6 hundreds

2 tens × 7 = 14 tens

6 hundreds + 1 hundred = 7 hundreds

Is there another way to work out 37 × 24?

I multiplied 37 by 4 by doubling and doubling again.

37 × 2 = 74
37 × 4 = 148

37 × 2 = 74
37 × 20 = 740

37 × 4 = 148
37 × 20 = 740
―――――――――――
37 × 24 = 888

37 × 2 = 74
37 × 2 tens = 74 tens

The florist uses 888 roses altogether to make the bouquets.

Practice

Multiply.

(a) 32 × 31 = ☐

32 × 1 = ☐

32 × 30 = ☐

(b) 23 × 24 = ☐

23 × 4 = ☐

23 × 20 = ☐

2. (a)
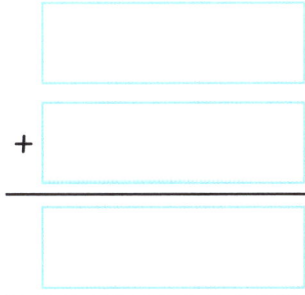

```
    3 7
×   2 6
-------
```

(b)
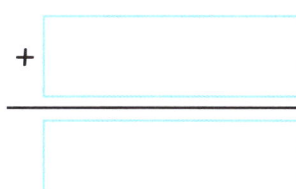

```
    4 8
×   3 9
-------
```

Dividing by 10, 100 and 1000

Lesson 13

Starter

In a warehouse, the packing team needs to put different items into boxes, packets and bags to be sent to a shop. The badges are put into boxes of 1000. The stickers are put into packets of 100. The key rings are put into bags of 10.
How many boxes, packets and bags can be filled?
Will there be any items left over in the warehouse?

Item	Number in stock
badges	3713
stickers	7692
key rings	2348

Example

Divide 3713 by 1000.

We can make 3 groups of 1000 from 3000.

3713 = 3000 + 713
3000 ÷ 1000 = 3

There will be 713 badges left over in the warehouse.

The packing team can fill 3 boxes of badges.

Next, divide 7692 by 100 to find the number of packets that can be filled.

7692 = 7000 + 600 + 92

We can make 70 groups of 100 from 7000.

We can make 6 groups of 100 from 6 hundreds.

7000 ÷ 100 = 70
600 ÷ 100 = 6

The packing team can fill 76 packets of stickers.

There will be 92 stickers remaining in the warehouse.

Divide 2348 by 10.

2348 = 2000 + 300 + 40 + 8
2000 ÷ 10 = 200
300 ÷ 10 = 30
40 ÷ 10 = 4

There will be 8 key rings remaining in the warehouse.

The packing team can fill 234 bags of key rings.

Practice

Divide.

1 (a) 500 ÷ 10 = ☐   (b) 2000 ÷ 10 = ☐

(c) 300 ÷ 100 = ☐   (d) 6000 ÷ 100 = ☐

(e) 2000 ÷ 1000 = ☐   (f) 9000 ÷ 1000 = ☐

2 (a) 2000 ÷ 20 = ☐   (b) 4000 ÷ 40 = ☐

(c) 100 ÷ 50 = ☐   (d) 1000 ÷ 50 = ☐

(e) 10 000 ÷ 50 = ☐   (f) 10 000 ÷ 1000 = ☐

Dividing 3-digit numbers

Lesson 14

Starter

There are 844 pupils at Mayfield School. The pupils are put equally into 4 house groups.
How many pupils are in each house group?

Example

844 ÷ 4 = ?

8 hundreds ÷ 4 = 2 hundreds

```
      2
4 ) 8   4   4
  - 8
    ─────────
        4   4
```

4 tens ÷ 4 = 1 ten

```
      2   1
4 ) 8   4   4
  - 8
    ─────────
        4   4
```

36

 4 ones ÷ 4 = 1 one

 Once 800 is divided by 4 we are left with 44.

Once 40 is divided by 4 we are left with 4.

We divide 4 by 4.

```
       2  1  1
   4 ) 8  4  4
     - 8
       ─────
          4  4
        - 4
          ─────
             4
           - 4
             ───
             0
```

844 ÷ 4 = 211

There are 211 pupils in each house group.

Practice

Divide.

1 696 ÷ 3 = ☐

```
   3 ) 6  9  6
```

2 448 ÷ 4 = ☐

```
   4 ) 4  4  8
```

3 882 ÷ 2 = ☐

```
   2 ) 8  8  2
```

Dividing 4-digit numbers

Lesson 15

Starter

There is a flight from Manchester to Dubai once a day.
Over a week, 5271 passengers flew to Dubai.
How many passengers were on each flight if the same number of passengers travelled each day?

Departures

Time	Flight	Destination	Gate	Status
12:20	CA 9234	Dubai	06	Departed
13:10	EZ 67	Sydney	10	Gate closed
13:25	AL 089	Perth	09	Final call
13:40	BA 2909	Hong Kong	11	Boarding now
14:50	SA 100	Bangkok	08	
15:45	VA 4017	Melbourne	01	
17:20	EZ 081	Brisbane	15	

Example

5271 ÷ 7 = ?

There are not enough thousands to make 1000 groups of 7.

We need to divide 52 hundreds by 7.

7) 5 2 7 1   →   7) 5 2 7 1

```
        7
7 ) 5  2  7  1
   -4  9
       3  7  1
```

52 hundreds = 49 hundreds + 3 hundreds

49 hundreds ÷ 7 = 7 hundreds

```
        7  5
7 ) 5  2  7  1
   -4  9
       3  7  1
      -3  5
          2  1
```

37 tens = 35 tens + 2 tens

35 tens ÷ 7 = 5 tens

```
        7  5  3
7 ) 5  2  7  1
   -4  9
       3  7  1
      -3  5
          2  1
         -2  1
              0
```

21 ones ÷ 7 = 3 ones

There were 753 passengers on each flight.

Practice

Divide.

1 (a)

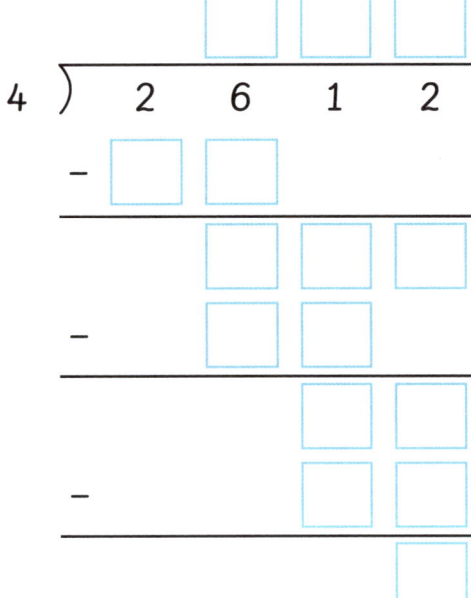

(b)

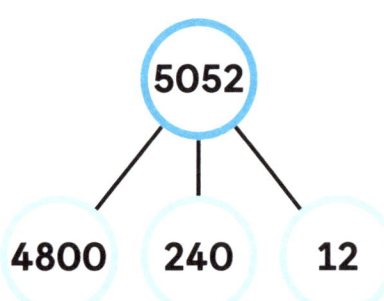

2 (a) 8) 2 7 9 2   (b) 3) 2 6 2 2

3 A cinema was full every night for a week. If 1169 people went to the cinema over the week and the same number of people went on each night, how many people went to the cinema on a single night?

☐ people went to the cinema on a single night.

Dividing with remainder

Lesson 16

Starter

Packets of microwave popcorn are put into boxes and delivered to shops. It takes 4 packets of popcorn to fill a box.
If a factory has 1453 packets of popcorn, how many boxes can it fill?
How many packets will remain at the factory?

Example

1453 ÷ 4 = ?

1453 = 1200 + 253

We can divide 12 hundreds by 4 exactly.

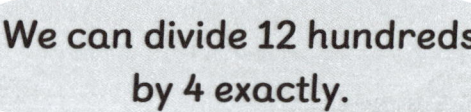

12 hundreds ÷ 4 = 3 hundreds

There are 2 hundreds remaining.

```
         3   6
    ┌─────────────
  4 │ 1  4  ²5  3
```

So, 2 hundreds and 5 tens become 25 tens.

 25 tens = 24 tens + 1 ten

24 tens ÷ 4 = 6 tens

```
      3 6 3 r 1
4 ) 1 4 ²5 ¹3
```

 The remaining 1 ten and 3 ones become 13 ones.

13 ones = 12 ones + 1 one

 12 ÷ 4 = 3

1453 ÷ 4 = 363 remainder 1

The factory can fill 363 boxes. One packet will remain at the factory.

Practice

Divide.

1 3) 1 2 3 7

2 4) 1 6 5 8

3 3) 1 1 4 7

4 6) 2 7 4 6

Review and challenge

1 Write the next 4 multiples of 7.

7, 14, 21, ☐ , ☐ , ☐ , ☐

2 List the factors of 32.

3 Find the common factors of 12 and 36.

4 Circle the prime numbers.

18   45   11   31   56   3   17

5 Write the first 5 square numbers greater than 2.

6 Write the first 3 cube numbers greater than 2.

7 Fill in the blanks.

(a) 13 × 10 = ☐

(b) 24 × 100 = ☐

(c) 8 × 1000 = ☐

(d) 73 × 1000 = ☐

8 Multiply.

(a) 213 × 2 = ☐

(b) 1332 × 3 = ☐

9 Divide.

(a) 884 ÷ 2 = ☐

(b) 996 ÷ 3 = ☐

10 Multiply.

(a)
```
      3 4
  ×   2 1
  _____
```

(b)
```
      4 6
  ×   3 4
  _____
```

11 Divide.

(a) 4) 8 5 6

(b) 7) 1 7 9 5 r ☐

Answers

Page 5 1 (a–b)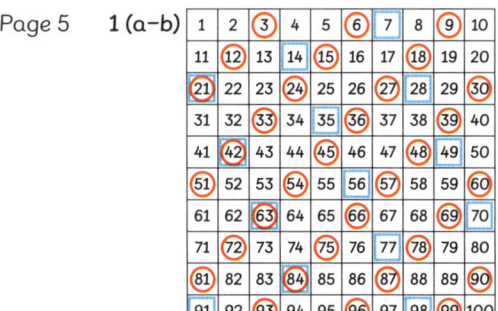

2 (a) 4, 8, 12, 16, 20, 24, 28, 32, 36, 40, 44, 48 (b) 6, 12, 18, 24, 30, 36, 42, 48, 54, 60, 66, 72 3 (b) 6 is a multiple of 1, 2, 3 and 6. (c) 10 is a multiple of 1, 2, 5 and 10.

Page 7 1 (a) 8 × 1 = 8, 4 × 2 = 8, 2 × 4 = 8, 1 × 8 = 8. The factors of 8 are 1, 2, 4 and 8. (b) 14 × 1 = 14, 7 × 2 = 14, 2 × 7 = 14, 1 × 14 = 14. The factors of 14 are 1, 2, 7 and 14. (c) Possible answers: 3 × 7 = 21, 1 × 21 = 21, 7 × 3 = 21, 21 × 1 = 21. The factors of 21 are 1, 3, 7 and 21. 2 (a) The factors of 18 are 1, 2, 3, 6, 9 and 18. (b) The factors of 16 are 1, 2, 4, 8 and 16.

Page 9 1 (a) The factors of 24 are 1, 2, 3, 4, 6, 8, 12 and 24. (b) The factors of 32 are 1, 2, 4, 8, 16 and 32. (c) The common factors of 24 and 32 are 1, 2, 4 and 8. 2 (a) Answers will vary. For example: 16, 24, 32 (b) Answers will vary. For example: 30, 60, 90

Page 11 1 (a) The factors of 8 are 1, 2, 4 and 8. (b) The factors of 16 are 1, 2, 4, 8 and 16. (c) The factors of 13 are 1 and 13. 2 Answers will vary. For example: 3, 5, 7 3 Answers will vary. For example: 4, 9, 16

Page 13 1 (c) $3^2 = 3 \times 3 = 9$ (d) $4^2 = 4 \times 4 = 16$ (e) $5^2 = 5 \times 5 = 25$ (f) $8^2 = 8 \times 8 = 64$ (g) $10^2 = 10 \times 10 = 100$

Page 15 1 $4 \times 4 \times 4 = 4^3 = 64$. There are 64 smaller cubes in this large cube. 2 (a) $1^3 = 1 \times 1 \times 1 = 1$ (b) $2^3 = 2 \times 2 \times 2 = 8$ (c) $3^3 = 3 \times 3 \times 3 = 27$ (d) $4^3 = 4 \times 4 \times 4 = 64$ (e) $5^3 = 5 \times 5 \times 5 = 125$ (f) $6^3 = 6 \times 6 \times 6 = 216$

Page 17 1 (a) 7 × 100 = 700

th	h	t	o
	7	0	0

(b) 9 × 1000 = 9000

th	h	t	o
9	0	0	0

2 (a) 13 × 10 = 130 (b) 27 × 100 = 2700 (c) 14 × 1000 = 14 000 (d) 234 × 1000 = 234 000

Page 20 1 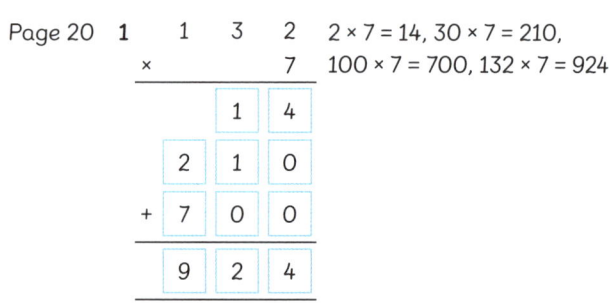 2 × 7 = 14, 30 × 7 = 210, 100 × 7 = 700, 132 × 7 = 924

2 (a) 147 × 3 = 441 (b) 216 × 4 = 864
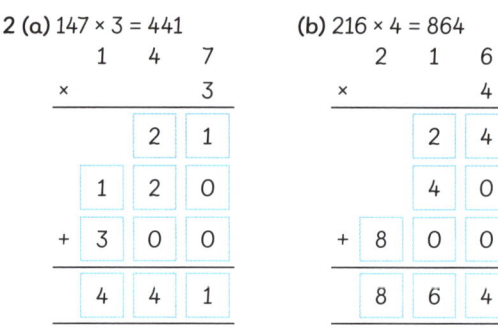

Page 21 3 The garden centre uses 1155 l of water in a week.

4 There are 1168 passengers on the train altogether.

Page 24 1 (a) 2131 × 2 = 4262, 1 × 2 = 2, 30 × 2 = 60, 100 × 2 = 200, 2000 × 2 = 4000 (b) 3123 × 3 = 9369, 3 × 3 = 9, 20 × 3 = 60, 100 × 3 = 300, 3000 × 3 = 9000

Page 25 2 (a) 2122 × 4 = 8488

46

(b) 3323 × 3 = 9969

```
      3  3  2  3
   ×           3
   ─────────────
               9
            6  0
         9  0  0
 +    9  0  0  0
   ─────────────
      9  9  6  9
```

3 (a) 1223 × 3 = 3669

```
      1  2  2  3
   ×           3
   ─────────────
               9
            6  0
         6  0  0
 +    3  0  0  0
   ─────────────
      3  6  6  9
```

(b) 4233 × 2 = 8466

```
      4  2  3  3
   ×           2
   ─────────────
               6
            6  0
         4  0  0
 +    8  0  0  0
   ─────────────
      8  4  6  6
```

(c) 3021 × 3 = 9063

```
      3  0  2  1
   ×           3
   ─────────────
               3
            6  0
         0  0  0
 +    9  0  0  0
   ─────────────
      9  0  6  3
```

(d) 2012 × 4 = 8048

```
      2  0  1  2
   ×           4
   ─────────────
               8
            4  0
         0  0  0
 +    8  0  0  0
   ─────────────
      8  0  4  8
```

Page 29   1 (a) 1426 × 3 = 4278, 1000 × 3 = 3000, 400 × 3 = 1200, 20 × 3 = 60, 6 × 3 = 18 (b) 2571 × 4 = 10 284, 2000 × 4 = 8000, 500 × 4 = 2000, 70 × 4 = 280, 1 × 4 = 4

2 (a)
```
      ⁵1 ²8 ⁵3  9
   ×           6
   ─────────────
      1  1  0  3  4
```
(b)
```
      ¹2 ⁵1 ²7  4
   ×           7
   ─────────────
      1  5  2  1  8
```

3
```
      ⁵1 ⁵9 ⁴8  7
   ×           6
   ─────────────
      1  1  9  2  2
```
The total mass of the 6 containers is 11 922 kg.

Page 31   1 (a) 31 × 11 = 341, 31 × 1 = 31, 31 × 10 = 310
(b) 23 × 13 = 299 2 (a) 44 × 12 = 528 (b) 33 × 22 = 726

Page 33   1 (a) 32 × 31 = 992, 32 × 1 = 32, 32 × 30 = 960
(b) 23 × 24 = 552, 23 × 4 = 92, 23 × 20 = 460

2 (a)
```
        ¹3 ⁴7
   ×     2  6
   ─────────
        2  2  2
   +    7  4
   ─────────
        9  6  2
```
(b)
```
        ²7 ⁷4  8
   ×        3  9
   ─────────────
           4  3  2
   +    1  4  4
   ─────────────
      1  8  7  2
```

Page 35   1 (a) 500 ÷ 10 = 50 (b) 2000 ÷ 10 = 200
(c) 300 ÷ 100 = 3 (d) 6000 ÷ 100 = 60 (e) 2000 ÷ 1000 = 2 (f) 9000 ÷ 1000 = 9 2 (a) 2000 ÷ 20 = 100
(b) 4000 ÷ 40 = 100 (c) 100 ÷ 50 = 2 (d) 1000 ÷ 50 = 20 (e) 10 000 ÷ 50 = 200 (f) 10 000 ÷ 1000 = 10

Page 37   1 696 ÷ 3 = 232
```
           2  3  2
      3 ) 6  9  6
        - 6
          ───
             9  6
          -  9
             ───
                6
             -  6
             ───
                0
```

2 448 ÷ 4 = 112
```
           1  1  2
      4 ) 4  4  8
        - 4
          ───
             4  8
          -  4
             ───
                8
             -  8
             ───
                0
```

3 882 ÷ 2 = 441
```
           4  4  1
      2 ) 8  8  2
        - 8
          ───
             8  2
          -  8
             ───
                2
             -  2
             ───
                0
```

47

Answers continued

Page 40 1 (a)
```
        6 5 3
    4 ) 2 6 1 2
      - 2 4
        ‾‾‾
          2 1 2
        - 2 0
          ‾‾‾
            1 2
          - 1 2
            ‾‾‾
              0
```

(b)
```
        8 4 2
    6 ) 5 0 5 2
      - 4 8
        ‾‾‾
          2 5 2
        - 2 4
          ‾‾‾
            1 2
          - 1 2
            ‾‾‾
              0
```

Page 41 2 (a)
```
        3 4 9
    8 ) 2 7 9 2
      - 2 4
        ‾‾‾
          3 9 2
        - 3 2
          ‾‾‾
            7 2
          - 7 2
            ‾‾‾
              0
```

(b)
```
        8 7 4
    3 ) 2 6 2 2
      - 2 4
        ‾‾‾
          2 2 2
        - 2 1
          ‾‾‾
            1 2
          - 1 2
            ‾‾‾
              0
```

3
```
        1 6 7      167 people went to the cinema
    7 ) 1 1 6 9    on a single night.
      - 7
        ‾
        4 6 9
      - 4 2
        ‾‾‾
          4 9
        - 4 9
          ‾‾
           0
```

Page 43 1
```
        4 1 2 r 1
    3 ) 1 2 3 7
```

2
```
        4 1 4 r 2
    4 ) 1 6 5 ¹8
```

3
```
        3 8 2 r 1
    3 ) 1 1 ²4 7
```

4
```
        4 5 7 r 4
    6 ) 2 7 ³4 ⁴6
```

Page 44 **1** 7, 14, 21, 28, 35, 42, 49 **2** 1, 2, 4, 8, 16, 32 **3** 1, 2, 3, 4, 6, 12 **4** 18, 45, ⑪, ㉛, 56, ③, ⑰ **5** 4, 9, 16, 25, 36 **6** 8, 27, 64

Page 45 **7 (a)** 13 × 10 = 130 **(b)** 24 × 100 = 2400 **(c)** 8 × 1000 = 8000 **(d)** 73 × 1000 = 73 000 **8 (a)** 213 × 2 = 426 **(b)** 1332 × 3 = 3996 **9 (a)** 884 ÷ 2 = 442 **(b)** 996 ÷ 3 = 332

10 (a)
```
        3 4
      ×   2 1
      ‾‾‾‾‾‾‾
        3 4
    + 6 8
      ‾‾‾‾‾‾‾
      7 1 4
```

(b)
```
      ¹ ²4 6
    ×   3 4
    ‾‾‾‾‾‾‾
      1 8 4
  + 1 3 8
    ‾‾‾‾‾‾‾
    1 5 6 4
```

11 (a)
```
        2 1 4
    4 ) 8 5 ¹6
```

(b)
```
        2 5 6 r 3
    7 ) 1 7 ³9 ⁴5
```